# What You Need

Before you get started, you'll need the following things.

## Scissors

Find a sharp pair of scissors to cut your threads. Ask an adult to help you.

## Embroidery threads

There is enough thread to make the first 10 bracelets in the book. You can find more in a local craft store.

## Ruler

A 12-in ruler is perfect.

## Board

Make your own bracelet board from strong cardstock, or use a clipboard if you have one.

## Binder Clip

Use a binder clip to attach your bracelet to your homemade board.

## Tape

You don't have to use a board! Stick the ends of your thread to the edge of a flat surface, like a table, with a piece of tape.

D1402503

# How this Book Works

A key appears at the top of the page for every new bracelet design.

The thread colors you will need to match the design.

The number of threads of each color that you will need.

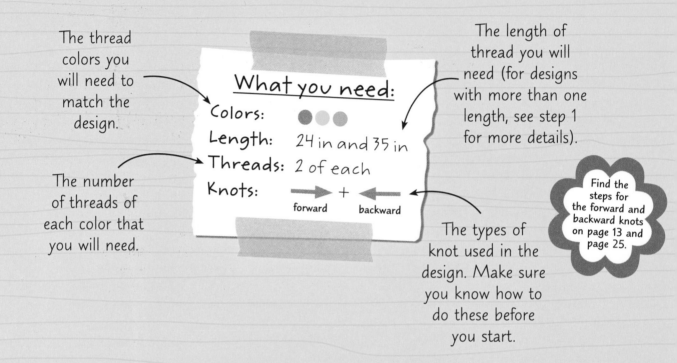

## What you need:

Colors:

Length: 24 in and 35 in

Threads: 2 of each

Knots: ⟶ forward + ⟵ backward

The length of thread you will need (for designs with more than one length, see step 1 for more details).

Find the steps for the forward and backward knots on page 13 and page 25.

The types of knot used in the design. Make sure you know how to do these before you start.

---

Each bracelet step has a diagram with instructions below it.

This is the top of your bracelet, where it is attached to the board.

The circles represent knots. For bracelets that use both types of knot, you'll notice that the circles are shown as different sizes.

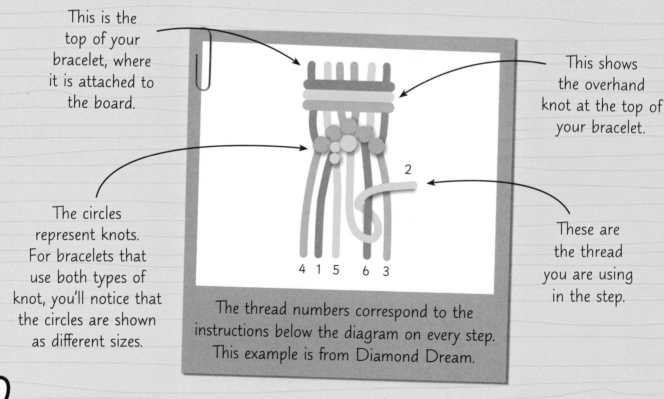

2

4 1 5 6 3

The thread numbers correspond to the instructions below the diagram on every step. This example is from Diamond Dream.

This shows the overhand knot at the top of your bracelet.

These are the thread you are using in the step.

# Bracelet Basics

Follow these steps for every bracelet design.

**1.** Line up your threads and get them roughly into the order they need to be in (see step 1 of each bracelet design).

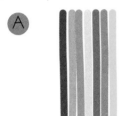

**A**

**2.** Knot all your threads together with one overhand knot, leaving about 2 inches of loose thread at the top.

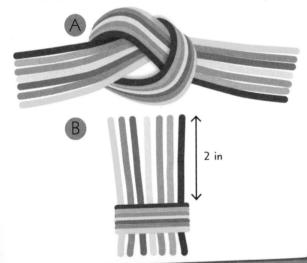

**A**

**B**

2 in

**3.** Attach the loose threads above your knot to the top of your board.

**4.** Separate your threads as shown in the step 1 diagram for each bracelet.

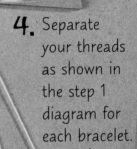

**5.** Once you have made a bracelet that is long enough for your wrist (about 5 inches should be enough), tie an overhand knot.

**6.** Finally, cut your threads leaving 2 inches of loose thread so that you can tie the bracelet onto your wrist.

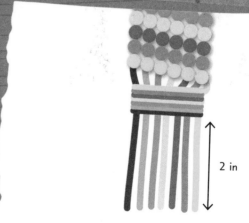

2 in

# Friendship Braid

This super-simple braid is really easy to do. Why not make one for your best friend in their three favorite colors?

Remember to attach your threads to your board!

1 2 3

**1.** Knot together your threads.

A B

2 1 3    2 3 1

**2.** To begin braiding, place thread 1 over thread 2, as A, then thread 3 over thread 1, as B.

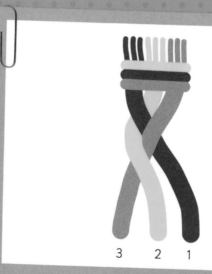

3 2 1

**3.** Now place thread 2 over thread 3.

Try making more bracelets with lots of different color combinations. Then layer them up on your wrists!

6

3   1   2

**4.** Then place thread 1 over thread 2.

Tighten the thread after each step.

1   3   2

**5.** Place thread 3 over thread 1.

1   2   3

**6.** Finally place the thread 2 over thread 3.

**7.** Repeat steps 2 to 6 until the bracelet fits your wrist.

Leave 2 in of loose thread at the start and finish of your braid.

Wear your handmade bracelets with store-bought ones!

7

# Fishtail Braid

Now that you've done a simple plait,
try making this cute fishtail version.
It will totally impress your friends!

## What you need:
Colors: ●●●●●●
Length: 12 in
Threads: 2 of each

See page 5
for a reminder
of how to get
started.

1 2 3 4 5 6

**1.** Cut two lengths of each color and knot them together.

It is easier if you start by holding threads 1 to 3 in your left hand and threads 4 to 6 in your right hand.

2 3 1 4 5 6

**2.** To begin, place thread 1 over threads 2 and 3.

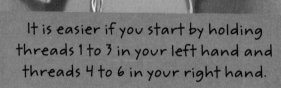

2 3 6 1 4 5

**3.** Next place thread 6 over threads 1, 4, and 5.

Remember to pull the thread tight after each step.

3 6   2 1 4 5

**4.** Place thread 2 over threads 3 and 6.

3 6 5   2 1 4

**5.** Place thread 5 over threads 2, 1, and 4.

Use more threads to get a chunkier bracelet, or three colors of threads for a different look!

6 5 3   2 1 4

**6.** Place thread 3 over threads 6 and 5.

6 5 4   3 2 1

**7.** Place thread 4 over threads 3, 2, and 1. The threads are now in reverse order.

9

To keep the braid tight, try to keep hold of all the threads.

5 4 6 3 2 1

**8.** Now place thread 6 over threads 5 and 4.

5 4 1 6 3 2

**9.** Place thread 1 over threads 6, 3, and 2.

4 1 5 6 3 2

**10.** Place thread 5 over threads 4 and 1.

4 1 2 5 6 3

**11.** Place thread 2 over threads 5, 6, and 3.

10

**12.** Place thread 4 over threads 1 and 2.

1 2  4 5 6 3

1 2 3  4 5 6

**13.** Finally place thread 3 over threads 4, 5, and 6. Repeat every step until the bracelet fits your wrist. Then tie a knot to finish.

## Learn how to braid your hair!

Long hair looks really pretty when it is braided, too! Just ask a friend or an adult to follow the bracelet steps using sections of your hair instead of threads!

See pages 6–7 for the steps to do a basic braid.

Part your hair into six sections to create the fishtail braid.

Split your hair into three sections to create the basic braid.

# Bracelet Designer

Create some new designs with bright colors,
then find the steps to make them for real!

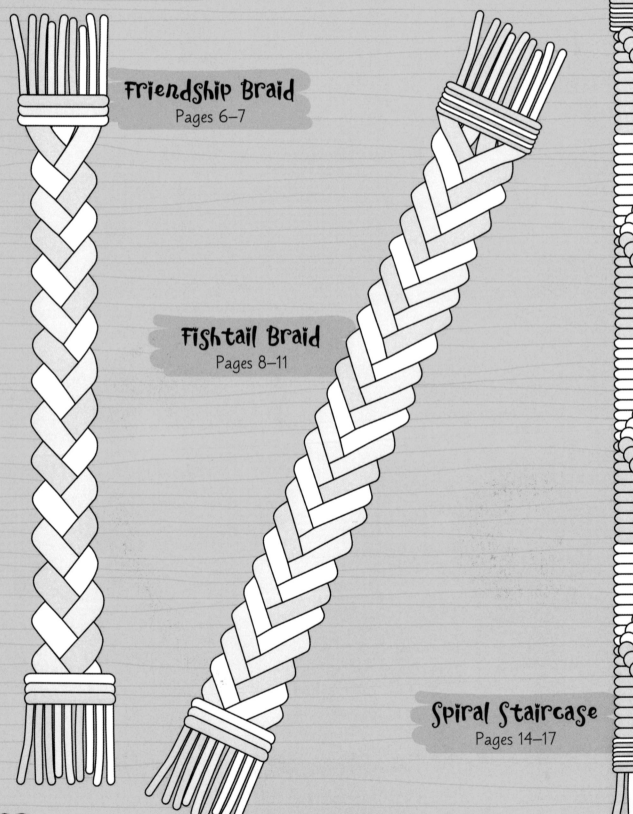

**Friendship Braid**
Pages 6–7

**Fishtail Braid**
Pages 8–11

**Spiral Staircase**
Pages 14–17

# How to tie a Forward Knot

The forward knot is simple to do. Learn how to do this technique first, then you'll be able to make amazing bracelet designs in no time.

**1.** Start by laying thread 1 over thread 2, to make a shape like the number 4.

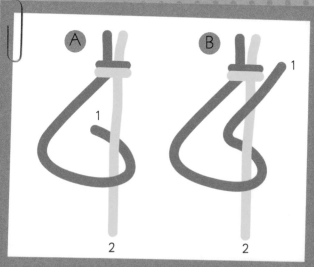

**2.** Next take thread 1 under 2, as A, then bring it up through the middle of the two threads, as B.

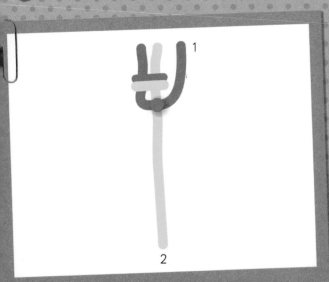

**3.** Pull thread 1 up to knot it tightly. You've completed a forward knot!

A double-forward knot is used in most bracelet designs—it is two forward knots, so follow these steps twice.

# Spiral Staircase

**What you need:**
Colors:
Length: 24 in
Threads: 1 of each
Knots: →

Let's get knotting! Start using your forward knot know-how to make this smart multicolored bracelet.

Go back to page 13 for a quick recap on the forward knot.

1 2 3 4 5 6 7

**1.** Cut a length of each thread and knot them together.

2 3 4 5 6 7

**2.** To start, use thread 1 to make a forward knot over all the other threads.

2 3 4 5 6 7

**3.** Make nine more forward knots with thread 1 over all the other threads, so you have completed 10 knots in total.

2 3 4 5 6 7 1

**4.** The knots will start to form the spiral. Unclip the threads from your board and turn your bracelet after every 10 knots.

34567    1

**5.** Next start a new color. Pull up thread 2 between threads 7 and 1.

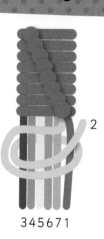

345671

**6.** Use thread 2 to make 10 forward knots over all the other threads.

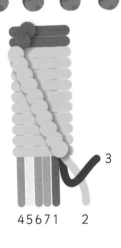

45671    2

**Remember to keep turning your bracelet!**

**7.** Pull up thread 3 between threads 1 and 2.

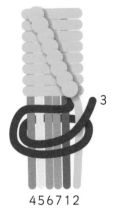

456712

**8.** Use thread 3 to make 10 forward knots over all the other threads.

Make a hair braid! Use longer lengths of thread to make a braid as long as your hair. Fasten the finished piece onto a barrette and put it in your hair.

56712    3

**9.** Pull up thread 4 between threads 2 and 3.

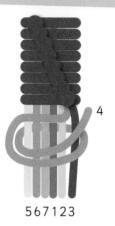

567123

**10.** Use thread 4 to make 10 forward knots over all the other threads.

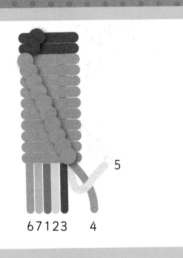

67123    4

**11.** Pull up thread 5 between threads 3 and 4.

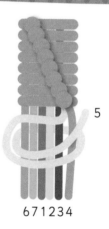

671234

**12.** Use thread 5 to make 10 forward knots over all the other threads.

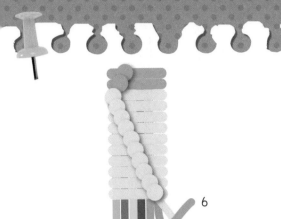

**13.** Pull up thread 6 between threads 4 and 5.

**14.** Use thread 6 to make 10 forward knots over all the other threads.

**15.** Pull up thread 7 between threads 5 and 6.

**16.** Use thread 7 to make 10 forward knots over all the other threads.

To make shorter color blocks, make five forward knots with each color.

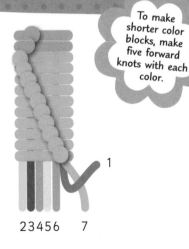

**17.** Finally start with thread 1 again! Pull it up between threads 6 and 7, then repeat steps 2 to 16 until the bracelet fits your wrist. Tie a knot to finish.

# Candy Shop

Turn these sweet treats into cute characters!

Candy colors look soooo cute on bracelet designs!

# Candy Color

Take inspiration from the Spiral Staircase bracelet and add colorful stripes to these candy canes.

# Candy Stripe

Once you've mastered the forward knot, try making this cute candy stripe bracelet! Just repeat the same technique with seven different-colored threads.

For a recap of the forward knot, go to page 13.

## What you need:
Colors:
Length: 24 in
Threads: 1 of each
Knots: ⟶

1 2 3 4 5 6 7

**1.** Cut a length of each thread and knot them together.

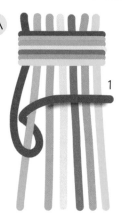 

A          B

2  3 4 5 6 7     2  3 4 5 6 7

**2.** Make a forward knot with thread 1 over thread 2, as A. Then do another forward knot with thread 1 over thread 2, as B. This is the double-forward knot.

2   3   4  5 6 7

**3.** Next make a double-forward knot with thread 1 over thread 3.

2 3 4 5 6 7

**4.** Then make a double-forward knot with thread 1 over thread 4.

1

2 3 4 5 6 7

**5.** Make a double-forward knot with thread 1 over thread 5.

1

2 3 4 5 6 7

**6.** Make a double-forward knot with thread 1 over thread 6.

1

2 3 4 5 6 7

**7.** Make a double-forward knot with thread 1 over thread 7. You have now completed the first row.

Each colored row becomes a stripe in your candy pattern!

2 3 4 5 6 7 1

**8.** Your threads should now be in this order.

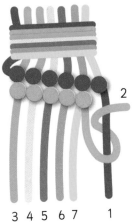

3 4 5 6 7    1

**9.** Now using thread 2, make a double-forward knot over each of the threads, from left to right—3, 4, 5, 6, 7, 1.

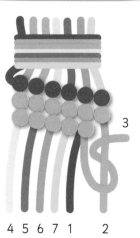

4 5 6 7 1    2

**10.** Next use thread 3 to make a double-forward knot over each thread, again, from left to right—4, 5, 6, 7, 1, 2.

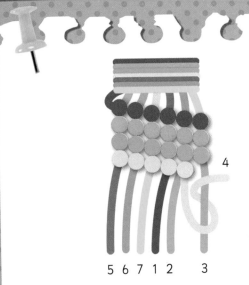

5 6 7 1 2    3

**11.** Use thread 4 to make a double-forward knot over each thread—5, 6, 7, 1, 2, 3.

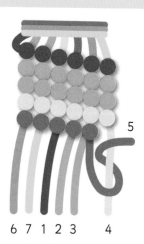

6 7 1 2 3    4

**12.** Use thread 5 to make a double-forward knot over each thread—6, 7, 1, 2, 3, 4.

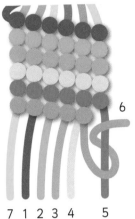

7 1 2 3 4 5

**13.** Use thread 6 to make a double-forward knot over each thread—7, 1, 2, 3, 4, 5.

1 2 3 4 5 6

**14.** Use thread 7 to make a double-forward knot over each thread—1, 2, 3, 4, 5, 6.

*Remember to keep making your knots from left to right.*

1 2 3 4 5 6 7

**15.** The threads should be back in the order they were at the start. You can now repeat steps 2 to 14 until the bracelet fits your wrist, then tie a knot to finish.

If you'd like to make a thinner bracelet, use just four or five threads instead of seven.

23

# Bracelet Designer

Use the templates to test out designs with your favorite colors.

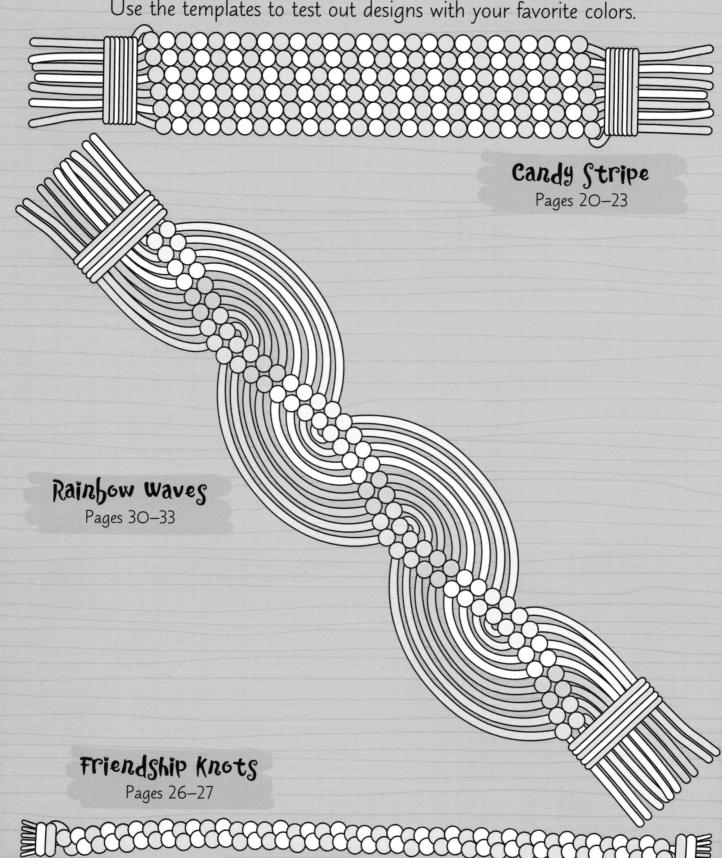

## Candy Stripe
Pages 20–23

## Rainbow Waves
Pages 30–33

## Friendship Knots
Pages 26–27

# How to Tie a Backward Knot

The backward knot technique is just like the forward kind—only the other way around! Practice it before you try the Friendship Knots bracelet on the next page.

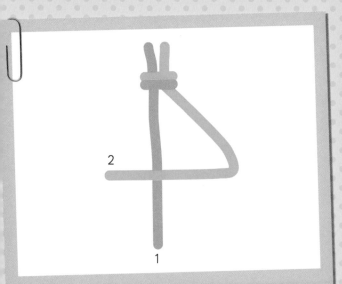

**1.** Start by laying thread 2 over thread 1, to make a shape like a backward number 4.

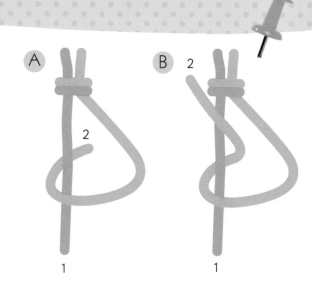

**2.** Next take thread 2 under 1, as A, then bring it up through the middle of the two threads, as B.

Backward knots are used with forward knots to create lots of different bracelet designs.

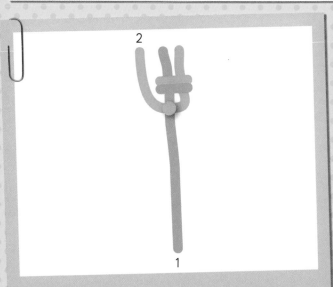

**3.** Pull thread 2 up to knot it tightly. You've completed a backward knot!

# Friendship Knots

Practice your forward and backward knots with this super-quick design.

Go to page 13 for the forward knot how-to and page 25 for the backward knot how-to.

## What you need:

Colors: ●●
Length: 24 in
Threads: 3 of each
Knots: ➡ + ⬅

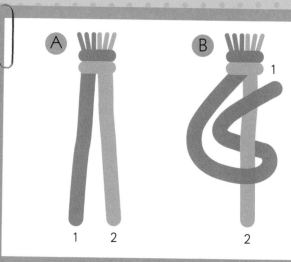

**1.** Knot together all the threads, as A. Then make a forward knot with thread 1 over thread 2, as B.

**2.** Use thread 1 again to make a backward knot over thread 2.

**3.** Now take thread 2 and make a backward knot over thread 1.

**4.** Take thread 2 again and make a forward knot over thread 1.

**5.** Repeat steps 1B to 4 until the bracelet fits your wrist. Tie a knot to finish.

## Making other jewelry!

You can follow the steps for any design to make all sorts of different jewelry items. Just use the guides here for the thread lengths.

To make a ring, use half the length of thread you would normally use for a bracelet.

To make a necklace, use three times the length of thread.

For an anklet, use two times the length of thread.

# My Style Quiz

Take this quiz to work out which bracelet would suit your style best.

## Question 1:
### Which pattern do you like the most?

A.
B.
C.

## Question 2:
### Complete this sentence:
### I can't live without my . . .

**A.** . . . striped T-shirt.
**B.** . . . locket necklace.
**C.** . . . patterned leggings.

## Question 3:
### What style do you rock the most?

**A.** Tomboy cool
**B.** Cute and girly
**C.** I don't have a set style

## Question 4:
### What color is your bedroom?

A. B. C.

Your style is relaxed and cheery, just like you. Make yourself the bright and bold Spiral Staircase bracelet (pages 14–17).

### Mostly As

You're known for your sweet and girly style, and happy-go-lucky nature. The Candy Stripe bracelet is perfect for you (pages 20–23).

### Mostly Bs

You're bags of fun and are not afraid to try new things. Let out your adventurous side with the Rainbow Waves bracelet (pages 30–33).

### Mostly Cs

# My Best Friend

Doodle your best friend in the frame. Then make them a bracelet!

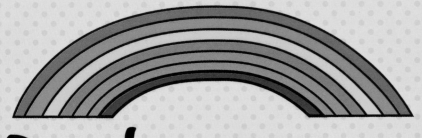

# Rainbow Waves

This colorful wave bracelet looks mega-impressive but it's actually pretty simple to do—give it a go!

## What you need:

Colors:
Length: 24 in (blue 12 in)
Threads: 2 of each
Knots: → + ←

**Threads 9 and 10 won't show on the finished design.**

1 2 3 4 5 6 7 8 9 10

**1.** Cut threads 1 to 8 at 24 in and threads 9 and 10 at 12 in, then knot together.

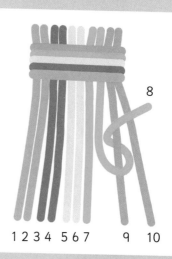

8

1 2 3 4 5 6 7  9  10

**2.** To start, make a double-forward knot with thread 8 over thread 9.

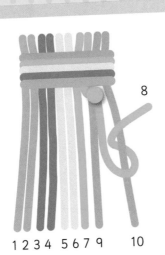

8

1 2 3 4 5 6 7 9  10

**3.** Next do a double-forward knot with thread 8 over thread 10.

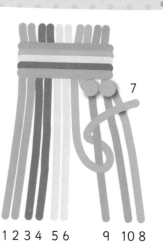

7

1 2 3 4 5 6  9  10 8

**4.** Make a double-forward knot with thread 7 over thread 9.

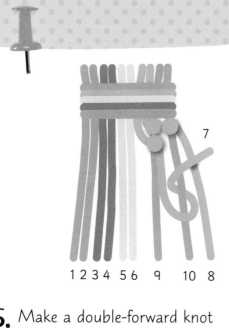

1 2 3 4 5 6   9   10   8

**5.** Make a double-forward knot with thread 7 over thread 10.

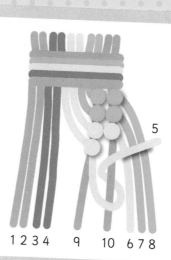

1 2 3 4   9   10   6 7 8

**6.** Make a double-forward knot with thread 6 over thread 9 then thread 10. Then do the same with thread 5.

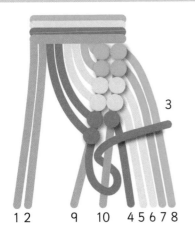

Paint your nails to match your rainbow arm candy!

1 2   9   10   4 5 6 7 8

**7.** Make a double-forward knot with thread 4 over thread 9 then thread 10. Then do the same with thread 3.

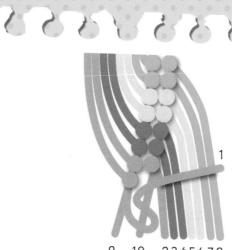

9   10   2 3 4 5 6 7 8

**8.** Make a double-forward knot with thread 2 over thread 9 then thread 10. Then do the same with thread 1.

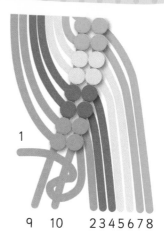

Don't pull the threads too tightly. It adds to the wave effect if they are looser!

1

9 10 2 3 4 5 6 7 8

**9.** Now go back the other way! Make a double-backward knot with thread 1 over thread 10.

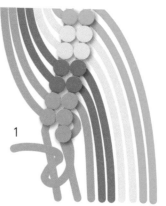

1

9 10 2 3 4 5 6 7 8

**10.** Next make a double-backward knot with thread 1 over thread 9.

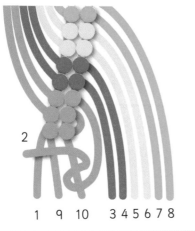

2

1 9 10 3 4 5 6 7 8

**11.** Then make a double-backward knot with thread 2 over thread 10.

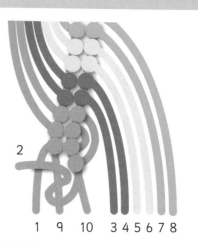

2

1 9 10 3 4 5 6 7 8

**12.** Make a double-backward knot with thread 2 over thread 9.

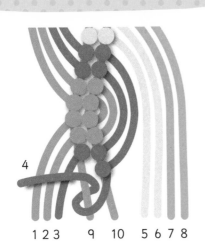

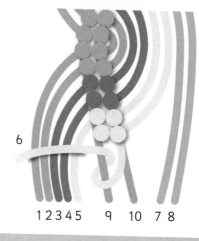

**13.** Make double-backward knot with thread 3 over thread 10 then thread 9. Then do the same with thread 4.

**14.** Make a double-backward knot with thread 5 over thread 10 then thread 9. Then do the same with thread 6.

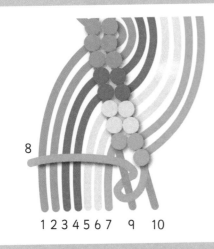

**15.** Make a double-backward knot with thread 7 over thread 10 then thread 9. Then do the same with thread 8.

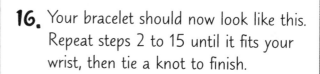
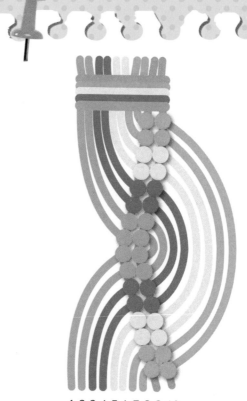

**16.** Your bracelet should now look like this. Repeat steps 2 to 15 until it fits your wrist, then tie a knot to finish.

This bracelet can be worn two ways—knotted side up (as shown in the steps) or the other way for the full wave effect!

33

# Crazy zigzag

The zigzag bracelet is a cute and funky design that everyone will love!

## What you need:

Colors:
Length: 35 in (pink 12 in)
Threads: 1 of each
Knots: ➡ + ⬅

> You won't see thread 5 once the bracelet is finished.

1 2 3 4 5

**1.** Cut threads 1 to 4 at 35 in and thread 5 at 12 in, then knot together.

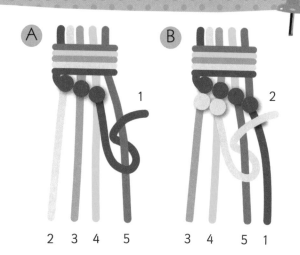

A

1

2 3 4 5

B

2

3 4 5 1

**2.** To start, make a double-forward knot with thread 1 over threads 2, 3, 4, then 5, as A. Make a double-forward knot with thread 2 over threads 3, 4, then 5, as B.

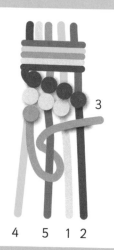

3

4 5 1 2

**3.** Make a double-forward knot with thread 3 over thread 4, then thread 5.

Create a whole armful of zigzag designs in lots of wacky colors to wear with your other jewelry.

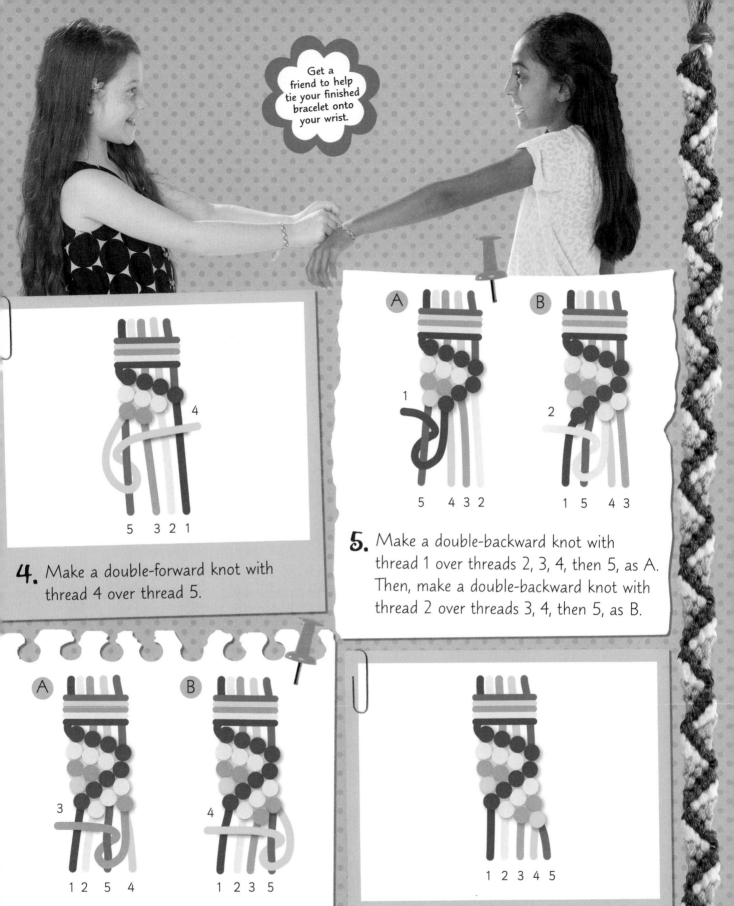

Get a friend to help tie your finished bracelet onto your wrist.

**4.** Make a double-forward knot with thread 4 over thread 5.

**5.** Make a double-backward knot with thread 1 over threads 2, 3, 4, then 5, as A. Then, make a double-backward knot with thread 2 over threads 3, 4, then 5, as B.

**6.** Make a double-backward knot with thread 3 over thread 4, then 5, as A. Finally, make a double-backward knot with thread 4 over thread 5, as B.

**7.** You should now be able to see the start of the zigzag pattern. Repeat steps 2 to 6 until the bracelet fits your wrist. Tie a knot to finish.

35

# Bracelet Designer

Here are more bracelets to color and complete!

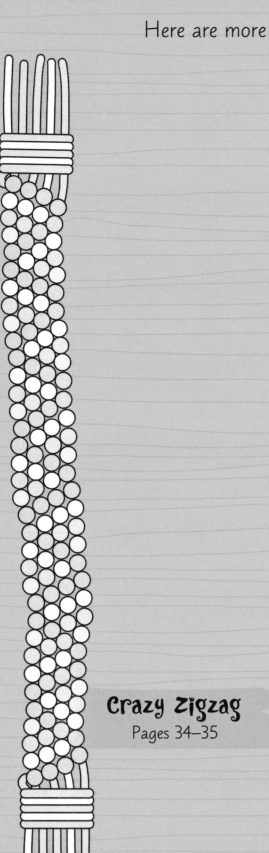

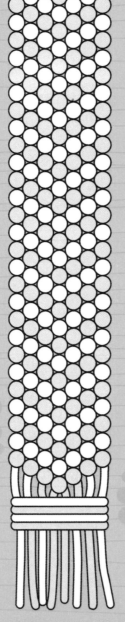

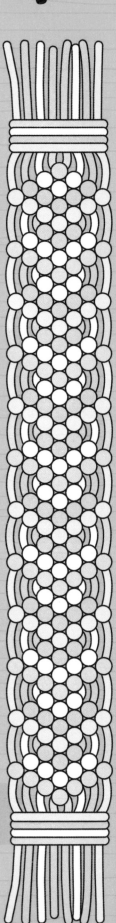

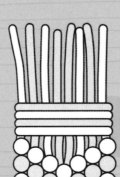

**Chic Chevron**
Pages 38–41

**Crazy Zigzag**
Pages 34–35

**Lovely Leaves**
Pages 44–47

# How to Add Beads to Bracelets

Learn how to attach beads to your bracelets and bling up your designs!
Beads can be added to any bracelet using either one of these two techniques.

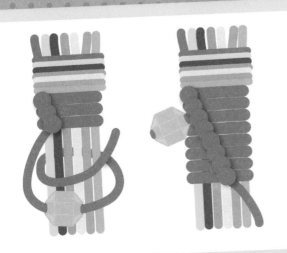

**1.** Thread a bead before a knot. Follow your bracelet steps as normal but add a bead onto the thread before making the knot (this example is the Spiral Staircase).

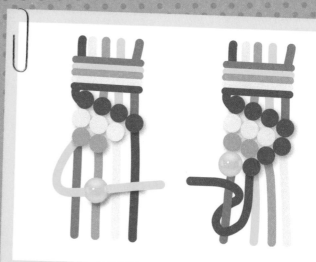

**2.** Use a bead instead of a knot. Follow the steps until you'd like to add a bead. Thread a bead on, then move to the next step (this example is the Crazy Zigzag).

ainbow Waves

Crazy Zigzag

Lovely Leaves

Spiral Staircase

# Chic Chevron

This neat pattern is a variation of the Candy Stripe design. You can alternate with two colors or pick four favorites.

## What you need:
Colors:
Length: 24 in
Threads: 2 of each
Knots: ➡ + ⬅

**1.** Cut two lengths of each thread and knot them together.

1 2 3 4 5 6 7 8

**2.** To start, make a double-forward knot with thread 1 over threads 2, 3, then 4.

2 3   4   5 6 7 8

1

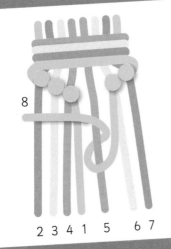

8

2 3 4 1 5   6 7

**3.** Make a double-backward knot with thread 8 over threads 7, 6, then 5.

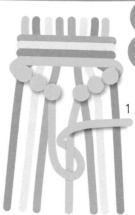

The middle knot will always use two threads of the same color.

2 3 4   8 5 6 7

1

**4.** Now make a double-forward knot with thread 1 over thread 8 so the threads switch places.

38

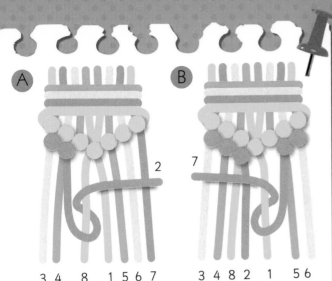

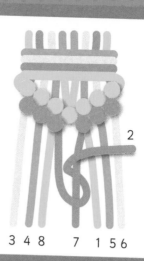

**5.** Make a double-forward knot with thread 2 over threads 3, 4, then 8, as A. Make a double-backward knot with thread 7 over threads 6, 5, then 1, as B.

**6.** Make a double-forward knot with thread 2 over thread 7.

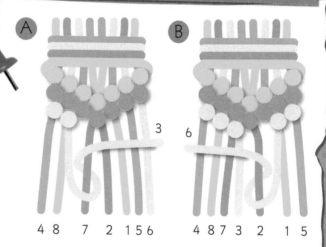

**7.** Make a double-forward knot with thread 3 over threads 4, 8, then 7, as A. Make a double-backward knot with thread 6 over threads 5, 1, then 2, as B.

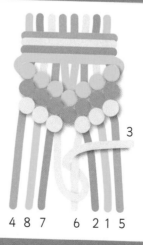

**8.** Make a double-forward knot with thread 3 over thread 6.

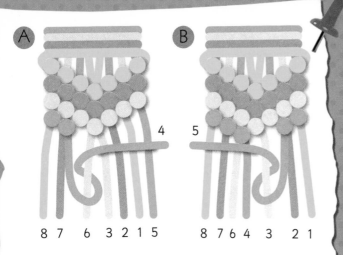

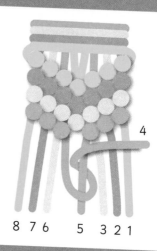

**9.** Make a double-forward knot with thread 4 over thread 8, 7 then 6, as A. Make a double-backward knot with thread 5 over threads 1, 2, then 3, as B.

**10.** Make a double-forward knot with thread 4 over thread 5.

Using different numbers of threads will change the thickness of your chevrons.

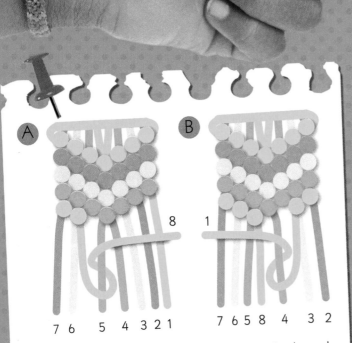

**11.** Make a double-forward knot with thread 8 over threads 7, 6, then 5, as A. Make a double-backward knot with thread 1 over threads 2, 3, then 4, as B.

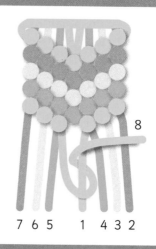

**12.** Make a double-forward knot with thread 8 over thread 1.

40

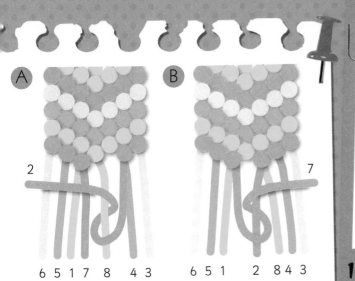

A

B

2

7

6 5 1 7 8    4 3       6 5 1    2 8 4 3

**13.** Make double-forward knots with thread 7 and then double-backward knots with thread 2, as A. Make a double-forward knot with thread 7 over 2, as B.

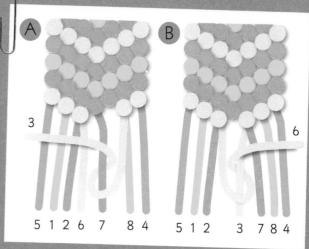

A

B

3

6

5 1 2 6 7    8 4       5 1 2    3 7 8 4

**14.** Make double-forward knots with thread 6 and then double-backward knots with thread 3, as A. Make a double-forward knot with thread 6 over 3, as B.

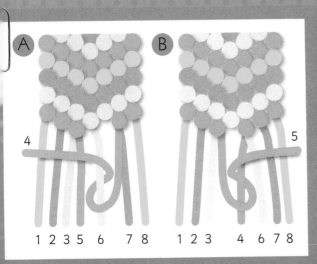

A

B

4

5

1 2 3 5  6   7 8       1 2 3   4 6 7 8

**5.** Finally make double-forward knots with thread 5 and then double-backward knots with thread 4, as A. Make a double-forward knot with thread 5 over 4, as B.

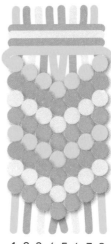

1 2 3 4 5 6 7 8

**16.** The threads are now back in the order they were at the start. Repeat steps 2 to 15 until the bracelet fits your wrist. Tie a knot to finish.

Making bracelets is fun to do as a group—why not have a bracelet-making party with your friends?

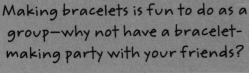

41

# Friendship Quiz

Use this handy quiz to decide which bracelet to make for your best friend. Start by choosing their favorite color thread.

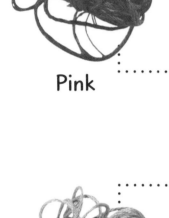

Pink

 Cute

What's their style?

Cool

Blue

Girly

What's their style?

Tomboy

 Fun

What's their style?

Quirky

 Purple

What's their favorite accessory? Barrette or Tiara

What's their favorite accessory? Backpack or sandals

What's their favorite accessory? Ring or purse

What's their favorite accessory? Hair elastic or cap

What's their favorite accessory? Pencil case or keyring

What's their favorite accessory? Sunglasses or watch

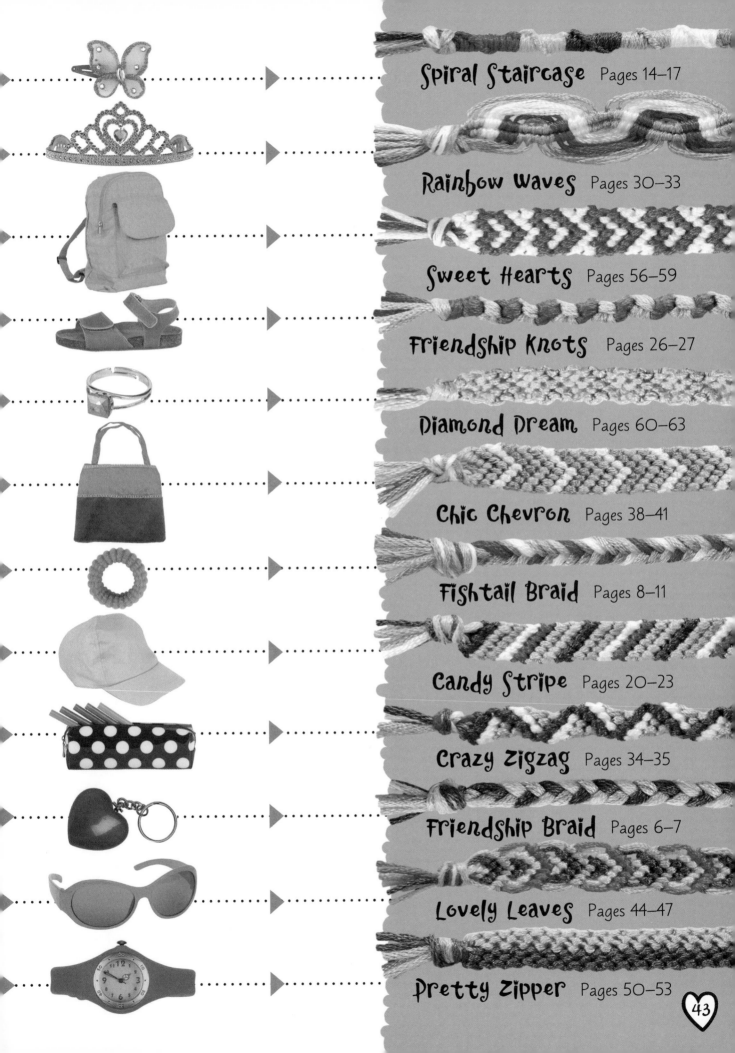

43

# Lovely Leaves

The knots on this bracelet design make a leaf pattern that looks super-special!

## What you need:
Colors: ● ● ● ●
Length: 24 in
Threads: 2 of each
Knots: ——➤ + ◄——

For a recap on a forward knot, see page 13.

1 2 3 4 5 6 7 8

**1.** Cut two lengths of each thread and knot them together.

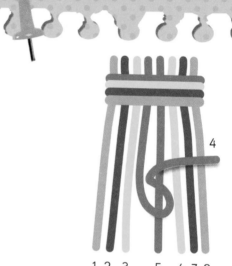

4

1 2 3  5  6 7 8

**2.** To start, make a double-forward knot with thread 4 over thread 5. The threads are the same color.

3

1 2  5  4 6 7 8

**3.** Make a double-forward knot with thread 3 over thread 5.

This design looks great with beads. See page 37 for the technique.

**4.** Make a double-backward knot with thread 6 over thread 4.

1 2 5 3 4 7 8

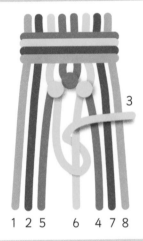

1 2 5 6 4 7 8

**5.** Make a double-forward knot with thread 3 over thread 6.

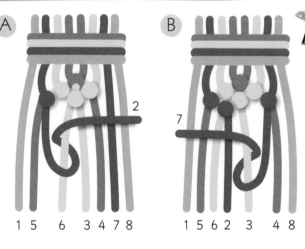

A

1 5 6 3 4 7 8

B

1 5 6 2 3 4 8

**6.** Next make a double-forward knot with thread 2 over thread 5, then 6, as A. Make a double-backward knot with thread 7 over thread 4, then 3, as B.

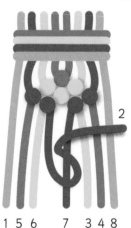

1 5 6 7 3 4 8

**7.** Make a double-forward knot with thread 2 over thread 7.

45

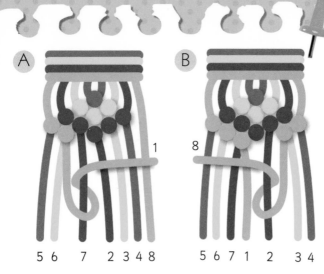

A      B

5 6   7   2 3 4 8      5 6 7 1   2    3 4

**8.** Next make a double-forward knot with thread 1 over threads 5, 6, then 7, as A. Make a double-backward knot with thread 8 over threads 4, 3, then 2, as B.

1

5 6 7    8   2 3 4

**9.** Make a double-forward knot with thread 1 over thread 8.

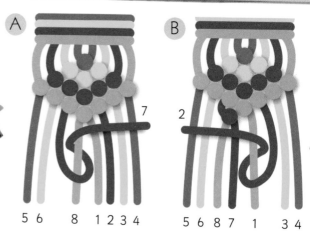

A      B

7      2

5 6    8   1 2 3 4      5 6 8 7   1    3 4

**10.** Make a double-forward knot with thread 7 over thread 8, as A. Then, make a double-backward knot with thread 2 over thread 1, as B.

7

5 6 8    2   1 3 4

**11.** Make a double-forward knot with thread 7 over thread 2.

Color combinations are endless!
Go crazy with bright colors
or make it pretty with pastel shades.

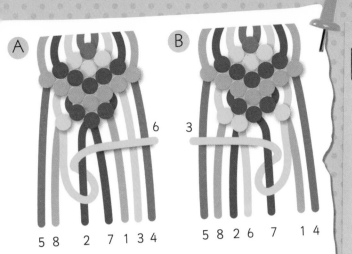

6   3

5 8   2   7 1 3 4      5 8 2 6   7   1 4

**12.** Make a double-forward knot with thread 6 over thread 8, then 2, as A. Then, make a double-backward knot with thread 3 over thread 1, then 7, as B.

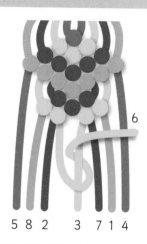

6

5 8 2   3   7 1 4

**13.** Make a double-forward knot with thread 6 over thread 3.

When you repeat the steps, remember threads 8 and 1 are now the opposite way around.

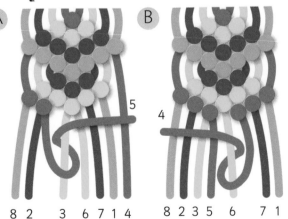

5   4

8 2   3   6 7 1 4      8 2 3 5   6   7 1

**14.** Make a double-forward knot with thread 5 over threads 8, 2, then 3, as A. Make a double-backward knot with thread 4 over threads 1, 7, then 6, as B.

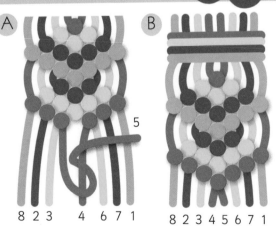

5

8 2 3   4   6 7 1      8 2 3 4 5 6 7 1

**15.** Finally make a double-forward knot with thread 5 over thread 4, as A. Then repeat steps 3 to 15 until the bracelet fits your wrist. Tie a knot to finish.

# Bracelet Designer

Pick pretty colors for these beautiful bracelet designs.

**Pretty Zipper**
Pages 50–53

**Sweet Hearts**
Pages 56–59

**Diamond Dream**
Pages 60–63

48

# How to Add a Pendant

Adding a pendant to your bracelet or necklace will make it an extra-special gift!
A pretty pendant can be added to any design—just follow the steps.

**1.** Pendants look best in the middle of a bracelet or necklace. Measure the length of one of your own bracelets or necklaces. Divide it in half and remember the length.

**2.** Follow the steps for your chosen design until it measures that length. Add your pendant onto one thread and continue following the steps.

For a necklace you'll need 3x the length of thread.

**3.** Finish your bracelet or necklace as normal, then turn it on its side so the pendant can hang as shown.

49

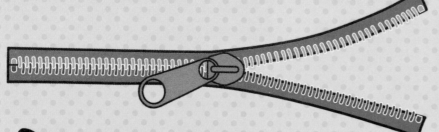

# Pretty Zipper

The knots in this bracelet make up a cool color-block design that is really eye-catching.

## What you need:

Colors:
Length: 24 in (blue 12 in)
Threads: 3 of each (1 blue)
Knots: ➡️ + ⬅️

*Thread 4 won't be seen on the final design.*

**1.** Cut the correct lengths of each thread and knot them together.

1 2 3 4 5 6 7

1

2 3 4 5 6 7

**2.** To start, make a double-forward knot with thread 1 over thread 2.

*For a bracelet with three colors, you'll need another hidden string to make knots onto.*

1

2   3   4 5 6 7

**3.** Next, make a double-forward knot with thread 1 over thread 3.

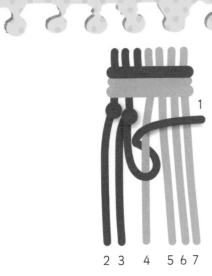

2 3  4  5 6 7

**4.** Then make a forward knot with thread 1 over thread 4.

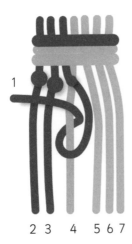

2 3  4  5 6 7

**5.** Now make a backward knot with thread 1 over thread 4.

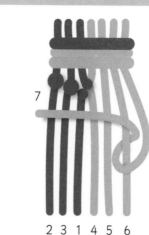

7

2 3 1 4 5 6

**6.** Next make a double-backward knot with thread 7 over thread 6.

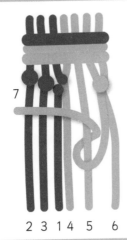

7

2 3 1 4 5  6

**7.** Make a double-backward knot with thread 7 over thread 5.

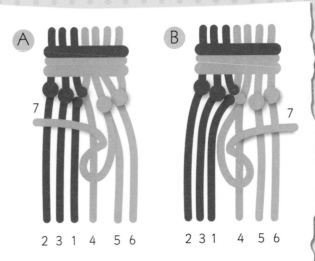

A 7

2 3 1 4  5 6

B 7

2 3 1  4 5 6

**8.** Make a backward knot with thread 7 over thread 4, as A. Make a forward knot with thread 7 over thread 4, as B.

51

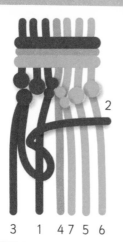

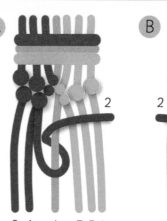

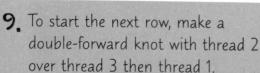
Always make your knots from the outside toward the center.

2

3 1 4 7 5 6

**9.** To start the next row, make a double-forward knot with thread 2 over thread 3 then thread 1.

A

B

2

2

3 1 4 7 5 6

3 1 4 7 5 6

**10.** Make a forward knot with thread 2 over thread 4, as A. Make a backward knot with thread 2 over thread 4, as B.

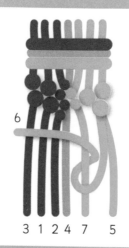

6

3 1 2 4 7 5

**11.** Now make a double-backward knot with thread 6 over thread 5 then 7.

A

B

6

6

3 1 2 4 7 5

3 1 2 4 7 5

**12.** Make a backward knot with thread 6 over thread 4, as A. Make a forward knot with thread 6 over thread 4, as B.

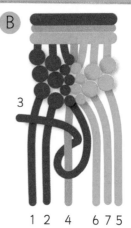

A

B

3

3

1 2 4 6 7 5

1 2 4 6 7 5

**13.** Make a double-forward knot with thread 3 over thread 1 then 2, as A. Make a forward knot and then a backward knot with thread 3 over thread 4, as B.

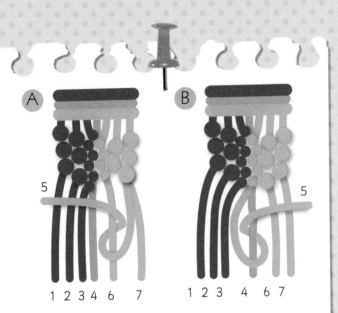

**A**

**B**

5

1 2 3 4 6 7

5

1 2 3 4 6 7

**14.** Finally make a double-backward knot with thread 5 over thread 7 then 6, as A. Make a backward then a forward knot with thread 5 over thread 4, as B.

1 2 3 4 5 6 7

**15.** The threads are now back in the order they were at the start. Repeat steps 2 to 14 until the bracelet fits your wrist. Tie a knot to finish.

## A rainbow of color!

At your local craft store, you'll find lots of different colors of embroidery thread to choose from.

Mixing up the colors makes the same design look really different!

Embroidery threads are coded by color so you can find the same thread again. The code can be found on the label.

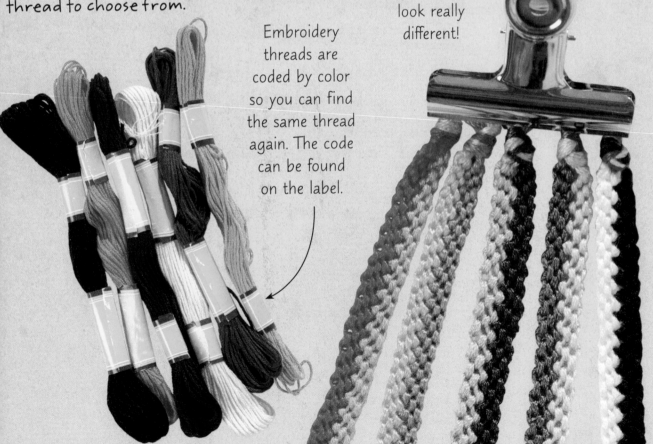

# Bracelet Doodle

Take a break from knotting to draw some bracelet designs!

Let's be best friends forever!

# My friendship tribe

Find out your friendship tribe and the bracelets that would suit all of you!
Pick each statement that is true for your group of friends.

- ✿ We always look out for each other
- ★ We like going on adventures
- ♥ We are all into fashion
- ✿ Everyone LOVES animals
- ★ There is a joker in our pack
- ♥ We LOVE anything sparkly

- ✿ We make sure everyone is included
- ★ It's always LOUD when we're around!
- ♥ We'd all be princesses if we could!
- ★ We can ALL keep a secret
- ✿ Everyone likes to party
- ♥ We like shopping together

## Mostly ★
Your group is full of fun and laughter. You bring out the best in each other, whatever situation you're in. Make the **Crazy Zigzag**!

(see pages 34–35)

## Mostly ✿
This is one tight-knit tribe! You are all caring, kind, and loyal. Everyone would like the **Lovely Leaves**!

(see pages 44–47)

## Mostly ♥
Your girly group is always wearing the latest fashions. Create the **Sweet Hearts** in colors to match your outfits.

(see pages 56–59)

# Sweet Hearts

This bracelet is one of the most complicated to make, but if you can master the steps, you'll wow your friends and family.

## What you need:
Colors:
Length: 35 in
Threads: 4 of each
Knots: ➡ + ⬅

**This bracelet uses a lot of thread. Make sure you have enough before you cut it!**

1 2 3 4 5 6 7 8

**1.** Cut four lengths of each thread and knot them together. Put a little tape around the ends of threads 1, 2, 7, and 8 will help you know which one is which.

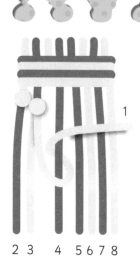

2 3   4   5 6 7 8

**2.** To start, make a double-forward knot with thread 1 over threads 2, 3, then 4.

8

2 3 4 1   5   6 7

**3.** Next, make a double-backward knot with thread 8 over threads 7, 6, then 5.

1

2 3 4   8   5 6 7

**4.** Now, make a double-forward knot with thread 1 over thread 8. These threads should be the same color.

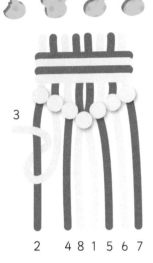

3

2    4 8 1 5 6 7

**5.** Then make a double-backward knot with thread 3 over thread 2 so that thread 3 ends up on the left.

6

3 2 4 8 1 5    7

**6.** Make a double-forward knot with thread 6 over thread 7 so that thread 6 ends up on the right.

A

2

3 4    8 1 5 7 6

B

7

3 4 8 2    1    5 6

**7.** Make a double-forward knot with thread 2 over thread 4 then 8, as A. Make a double-backward knot with thread 7 over thread 5, then 1, as B.

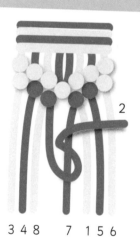

2

3 4 8    7 1 5 6

**8.** Next make a double-forward knot with thread 2 over thread 7. These threads should be the same color.

3    8 7 2 1 5 6

**9.** Now make a double-backward knot with thread 4 over thread 3 so that thread 4 ends up on the left.

4 3 8 7 2 1    6

**10.** Make a double-forward knot with thread 5 over thread 6 so that thread 5 ends up on the right.

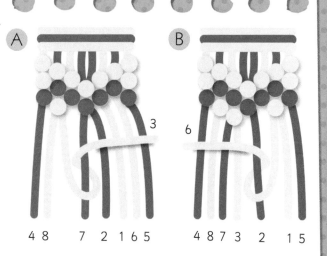

A

4 8    7  2 1 6 5

B

4 8 7 3   2    1 5

**11.** Make a double-forward knot with thread 3 over thread 8, then 7, as A. Make a double-forward knot with thread 6 over thread 1, then 2, as B.

4 8 7    6    2 1 5

**12.** Now make a double-forward knot with thread 3 over thread 6. These threads should be the same color.

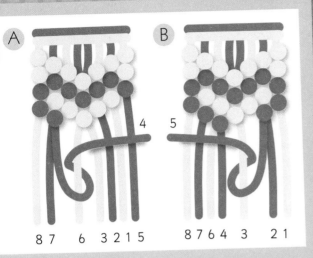

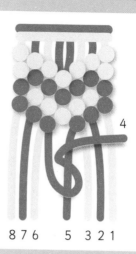

**13.** Make a double-forward knot with thread 4 over threads 8, 7, then 6, as A. Make a double-backward knot with thread 5 over threads 1, 2, then 3, as B.

**14.** Then make a double-forward knot with thread 4 over thread 5. These threads should be the same color.

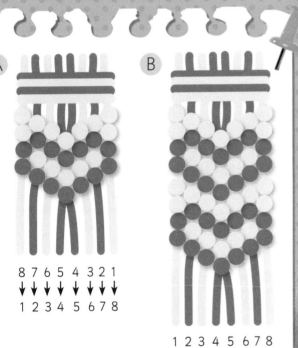

**15.** The threads are now in reverse order. Repeat steps 2 to 14 using thread 8 as 1, thread 7 as 2, and so on, as A. Your threads will then be back in the same order as when you started, as B.

**16.** Keep repeating until the bracelet fits your wrist, then tie a knot to finish.

Become bracelet twins with a friend! Each make a bracelet to match the other one's outfit.

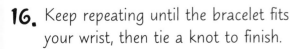

# Diamond Dream

This diamond design is created with a mix of knots and double knots. Stick to the steps and your bracelet will be beautiful!

**What you need:**
Colors: ●●●
Length: 24 in (pink 35 in)
Threads: 2 of each
Knots: → + ←

*Longer threads can get tangled. Keep an eye on your lengths!*

1 2 3 4 5 6

**1.** Cut threads 1, 2, 5, and 6 to 24 in and threads 3 and 4 to 35 in, then knot them together.

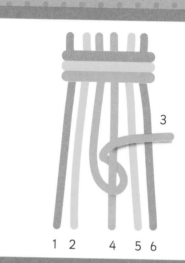

3

1 2 4 5 6

**2.** To start, make a double-forward knot with thread 3 over thread 4.

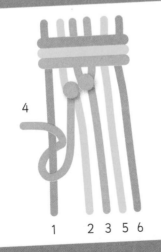

4

1 2 3 5 6

**3.** Make a double-backward knot with thread 4 over thread 2, then thread 1.

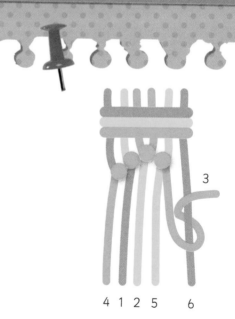

3

4 1 2 5 6

**4.** Then make a double-forward knot with thread 3 over thread 5, then thread 6.

**5.** Now make a double-forward knot with thread 2 over thread 5.

4 1   5   6 3

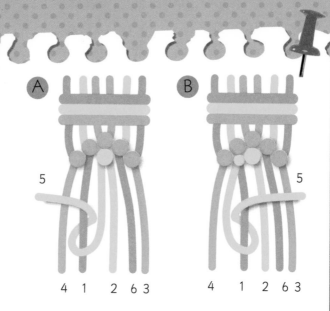

A   B

5                                                        5

4 1   2   6 3                        4   1   2   6 3

**6.** Make a backward knot with thread 5 over thread 1, as A. Make a forward knot with thread 5 over thread 1, as B.

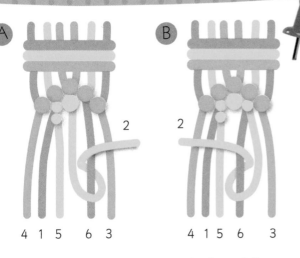

A                                B

2                        2

4 1 5   6   3                    4 1 5   6   3

**7.** Make a forward knot with thread 2 over thread 6, as A. Then, make a backward knot with thread 2 over thread 6, as B.

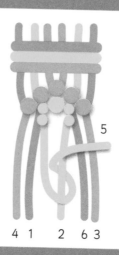

5

4 1   2   6 3

**8.** Now make a double-forward knot with thread 5 over thread 2.

Try using the same colored thread for 1, 2, 5, and 6, to get a different two-tone look.

**9.** Make a double-forward knot with thread 4 over thread 1, then over thread 2.

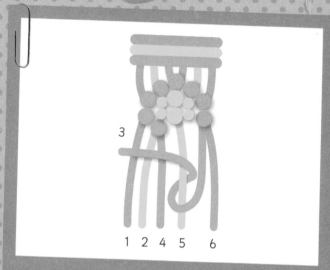

**10.** Make a double-backward knot with thread 3 over thread 6, then over thread 5.

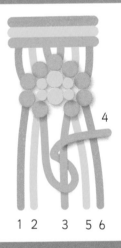

**11.** Make a double-forward knot with thread 4 over thread 3. The threads will look like they are back at the beginning, but there are a couple of steps to go.

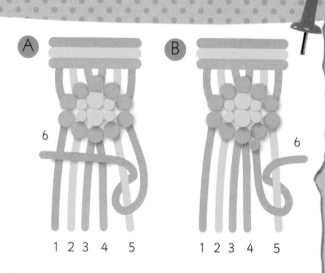

**12.** Make a backward knot with thread 6 over thread 5, as A. Then, make a forward knot with thread 6 over thread 5, as B.

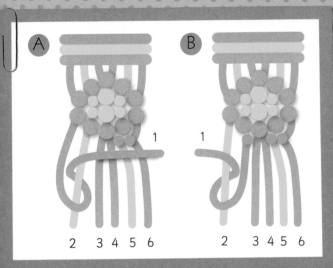

**13.** Make a forward knot with thread 1 over thread 2, as A. Then make a backward knot with thread 1 over thread 2, as B.

**14.** Your threads should now be back where they started. Repeat steps 2 to 13 until the bracelet fits your wrist, then tie a knot to finish.

## So many bracelets!

Now that you know how to make every bracelet design, why not make a whole collection in your favorite colors!

Remember, necklaces use more thread than a bracelet. Rings use less thread.

# Finishing touch

Try another way of finishing your bracelets—braid the ends.

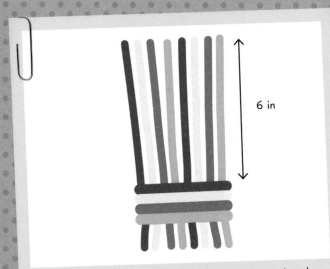

6 in

Add 8 in to the thread length given in the key before you start making your chosen design. Leave 6 in (instead of 2 in) before knotting your threads together.

Friendship Braid

Fishtail Braid

When you have finished your design, braid the loose thread at either end. Choose from either the **Friendship Braid** (pages 6–7) or the **Fishtail Braid** (pages 8–11).

## The Making of the Book

157 bracelets were made using over 874 yards of thread!

Every bracelet in this book was handmade by Nicola Friggens.

The 12 bracelet designs were beautifully worn by 16 models.

Over 1,000 photographs were taken over three days by Daniel Pangbourne.